A Blessed Big Day:
Collected Christmas Poems

By Ralph E. Brown

*To Sandra
with love
Ralph*

Doorlight Publications

Doorlight Publications
PO Box 718, South Hadley, MA 01075
www.doorlightpubs.com
info@doorlightpubs.com

©2011 Ralph E. Brown

All rights reserved. No part of this book may be reproduced in any form, except as permitted by US copyright laws, without written permission
from Doorlight Publications.

First published 2011 by Doorlight Publications.

Scripture quotations taken from the Holy Bible, New International Version® NIV®. Copyright ©1973, 1978, 1984 by International Bible Society. Used by permission of Zondervan Publishing House. All rights reserved.

Cover art by Allison Brown
Book Design: Allison Brown

ISBN 978-0-9778372-9-8
Printed in the United States of America

Contents

Condescension 3
The Christmas Story 5
Love has Come 7
The Messiah 9
When Angels Come 11
Christmas in Hyderabad 13
What is Christmas? 15
Stars and the Star 17
A Big Day in Pakistan 19
Only One 21
Christmas in Larkana 23
God Could Have Made Another Way 25
Light 27
Shepherds - Angels 29
Glory to God 31
Jesus Came! 33
When I Think of Christmas... 35
God Became Man 37
What If there Were no Christmas? 39
Christmas in Pakistan 41
Who was this Child? 43
Separation at Christmas 45
Remember Christ at Christmas 47
His Place and Ours 49
What is Christmas? 51
Christmas is a Time for Singing 53
"And He will be called... Price of Peace. Of the increase of His government and peacethere will be no end." (Is 9:7) 55
What does Christmas Mean to Me? 57
What Will the New Year Bring? 59
Christmas Carols 61
One Message – One Word 63
The Incarnation 65
Pain at Christmas 67

Author's Preface

For many years it has been my hobby to write a poem for our Christmas letter. Many of these were written while we were serving in the Sindh province of Pakistan. Oftentimes the poem was written hurriedly to meet a deadline. Most of the poems were centered on the Incarnation. Some concerned Christmas traditions.

I do not consider myself a poet. To my mind a poet is one who is far more gifted in the art of language than what I consider myself to be. I prefer to call myself a "rhymester" since I like rhyme, whether in light verse or serious and deep philosophy.

Several loved ones and friends have urged me to put my Christmas poem into a book. I am thankful to Doorlight Publications for agreeing to publish these poems. I hope that the great message of the Incarnation of Christ our Savior will emerge clearly to the reader. And I also hope that some of the verse will be used in worship, even some put to song, for some of the poems are singable.

I am grateful to my granddaughter, Ruth Anne Brown, for typing and formatting the poems. My loving thanks to my wife Polly who urged me to write a poem each Christmas season and for her encouragement and constructive criticism of the poems.

Thankful that Christ came, and He will come again.

Ralph E. Brown
Hadley, Massachusetts
February 2010

A Blessed Big Day

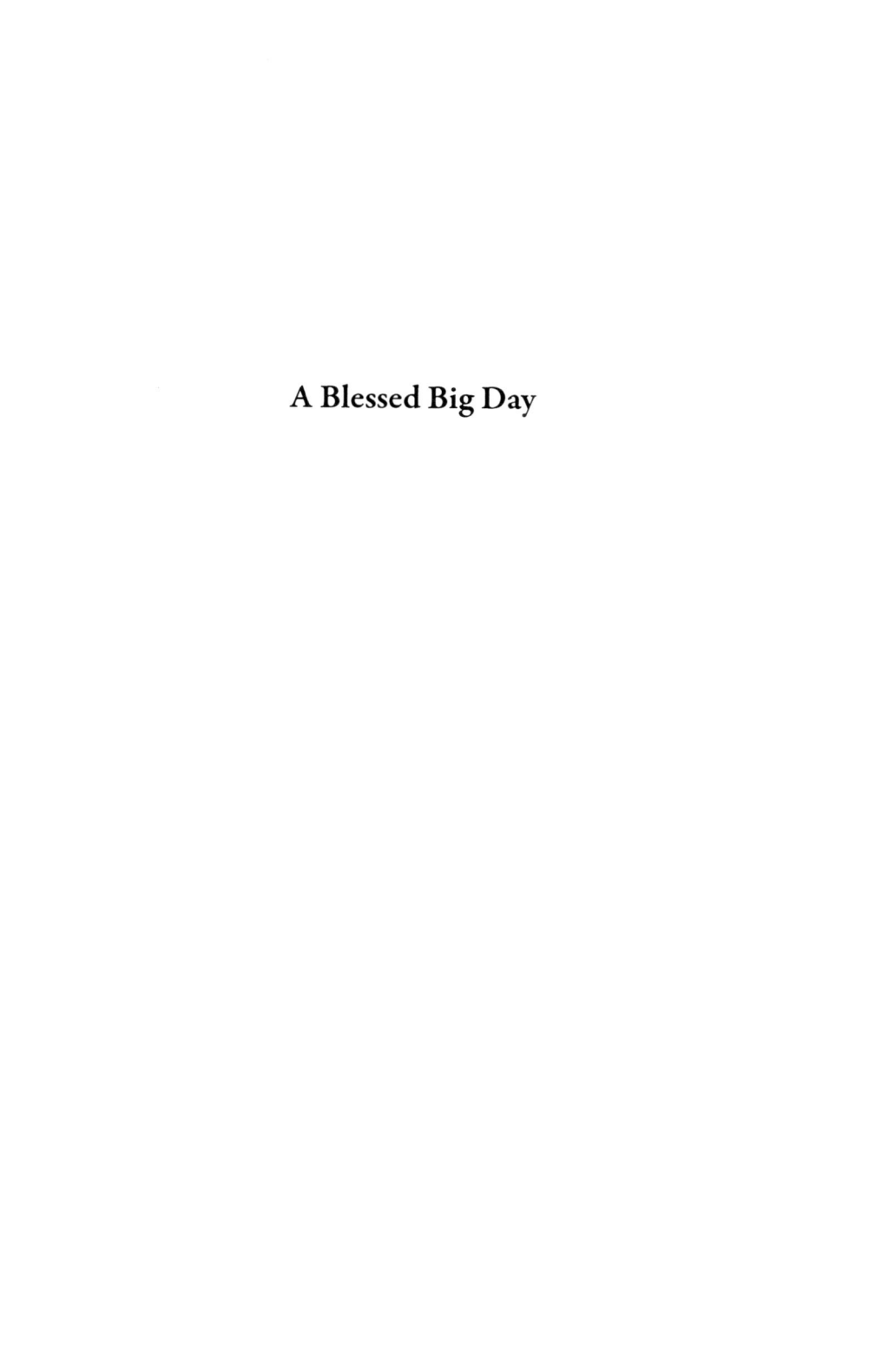

Condescension

1962

Amidst the season's joy and mirth
We remember the Messiah's birth
And ponder why He came.

From heav'n into a world of sin
To give us lasting peace within
Our Lord and Savior came.

From Father's home and loving heart
Becoming man in fullest part
The Son Incarnate came.

Leaving His throne and jeweled gate
Born as a babe in humble state
The King Eternal came.

From the dwelling of Eternal Light
To rid the world of sin's dark blight
The Light of Life so came.

Leaving the realm of endless day
To die a death that sinners may
Forever live – the Lord Christ came.

From Heaven – the place of peace and life
To show a world sore torn with strife
God's peace – Immanuel came.

He left it all, nor self did please
So why can't I forsake some ease
To tell men why He came? †

The Christmas Story

A Roman emperor decreed
A census must be made
To Bethlehem's town a couple came
Their debt to Rome was paid.

From Nazareth in Galilee
They traveled ancient ways,
Through hills which David loved so well
And spent his youthful days.

Midst the crowded Jewish town
They found no room but one,
A place where animals were stalled
To bear her first born son.

The virgin mother, tired and weak
A humble Jewish maid,
Wrapped the child in strips of cloth
Him in a trough she laid.

Shepherds waiting out the night
Watching their flocks of sheep
Startled by brightness in the sky
Their fear was real and deep.

They saw an angel from the Lord
Who brought good news of joy,
A Savior born that day in town
A little baby boy.

The angel called Him Christ the Lord
And to seal the claim,
Great throngs of heavenly beings sang
Glory to God's Name.

The Shepherds hurried off to see
What had taken place
And found the baby as was told,
The Savior of the race.

They spread the word of what they heard
To God they gave the praise
Lord, like them help us to tell
The Good News in these days. †

Love has Come
To the tune of "He is Lord"

1990

God is Love, God is Love,
And He sent His only Son to prove His Love
All the world should know,
Every People see
That God the Lord is Love.

He has come, He has come
He was born a little babe in Bethlehem.
Shepherds bowed their knees,
Wisemen gave their gifts
To worship God's dear Son.

He has come, He has come,
To dwell in human hearts, the Lord has come.
People must believe,
Lasting life receive
For Jesus Christ has come.

He has come, He has come,
To grant life and hope and peace the Christ has come.
God's good news for all,
Whether great or small
Immanuel has come.

He will come, He will come,
According to His promise He will come.
Spread the gospel wide,
Roll the Kingdom's tide
Before the Lord shall come. †

The Messiah
Jacobabad, 1965

The woman's seed
Destined to bruise the serpent's head
Laid in a manger for a bed
In God's own time did come.

From father Abraham
To bless all nations of the earth
The Christ child came of lowly birth
All men to reconcile.

Of Judah's tribe
From whom the scepter did not part
A Ruler sent from God's own heart,
Nations to him shall come.

From Jesse's roots
A branch on whom the Spirit came
Was born with an exalted name
Jesus, Savior from sin.

On David's throne
A king, whose reign shall have no end
Came first to die, the veil to rend
Then live forevermore.

A virgin's son
Immanuel His name to be
From heav'n incarnate Deity
God dwelling amongst men.

The son of God
Whom prophets long ago foretold
Would come to save me from sin's mold
Today my Lord and King. †

When Angels Come

1966

An angel came
A virgin maid to greet
And tell that she would bear a Son
To reign on David's seat.

An angel came
To Joseph carpenter brave
To tell him that the Child would be
Jesus – His race to save.

An angel came
To shepherds in the night
To tell them of the manger's Child.
Their hearts from fear took flight.

God's angels came
To tell men of Christ's birth
Yet Whom we worship and adore
Is more than angels' worth.

Angels will come
At His glory filled return
With all His holy angels.
Our hearts for Jesus yearn. †

Christmas in Hyderabad

1967

Children home from Boarding
Joining in the fun
Of the yuletide season
The term's schoolwork is done.

Mommy in the kitchen
Mixing up to bake
Nuts and raisins, date and peel
Another big fruit cake.

Poinsettia in the garden
Blooming big and tall
Once a tiny potted plant
A mali's gift to all.

Grammy here for Christmas
What a glad re-une
To see her after many months
She's going back too soon.

Daddy at the printer
Hoping and praying too
That the Christmas leaflets
Are off the press when due.

Family round the table
In happy holiday style
Addressing cards to friends and more
Across too many a mile.

Christmas time in Hyderabad
Remembering once again
Our Savior, Christ the Lord and King
Who came to save all men.

We send to you our Greetings
Along with prayer and Love
May the Christ for whom is Christmas
Enrich you from above. †

What is Christmas?
Hyderabad, 1968

What is the essence of Christmas
Which we celebrate year by year?
Is it having a holiday spirit
And wiping away every tear?

Is Christmas enjoying good health
Or reunion with loved ones at home?
Is it fellowship with our friends
Singing carols – reciting a poem?

Does snow on the ground make it Christmas?
Or a glittering evergreen tree?
New clothes to wear on the twenty fifth
The fruits of a mad shopping spree?

Is stuffed turkey the makings of Christmas
Or chickens, if turkey's not found?
Is it having the stocking filled to the top
And presents all scattered around?

Would peace in the world make it Christmas
If hearts were still bent to sin?
Or does the good spirit of giving
Bring Christmas to sinners within?

If Christmas means what one can do
Or is shaped by good health or clime
Then the essence of Christmas remains
With man and the fortunes of time.

No, Christ is Christmas' present
To a world which needs the Lord
And Christmas is "God with us"
To those who reflect on his word.

Knowing Christ is the essence of Christmas
Experiencing a birth from within
For the Babe of Bethlehem's manger
Is Jesus the Savior from sin. †

Stars and the Star

1969

A star shall come from Jacob (Numbers 24:17)
With scepter He shall reign
All that the prophets had foretold
Shall in Him be made plain.

The myriad stars He made (Ps. 8:3)
Which draw men to amaze
Though differing in glory (I Cor. 15:41)
With wonder show his praise. (Ps. 148:3)

The Offspring of David's line
The Bright and Morning Star (Rev. 22:16)
Was worshipped by some kingly men
Who traveled from afar. (Mt. 2:2)

The shining star of Bethlehem
Led them to the scene (Mt. 2:9)
Where God in history became man (Phil. 2:6,7)
As Savior – King supreme.

There is another star
Joined with a crescent moon
A symbol of the Muslim power
Across the desert dune.

Unless the Star of Jacob
Appears to shed his light
The star and crescent will remain
To keep souls in the night.

Another Christmas time
With tree and tinsel star
Lord, let them not make us forget
Lost ones both near and far. †

A Big Day in Pakistan
*In Pakistan when we say Happy Christmas,
we say "A Blessed Big Day"*

Christmas is a big day
For Christians in this land
In village hut or bungalow
In town or desert sand.

Christmas is a big day
It comes but once a year
A special time of happiness
For rich and poor to share.

Christmas is a big day
New clothes and special food
For even in the poorest homes
There is a festive mood.

Christmas is a big day
Homes, whitewashed and neat
And Christians travel far and near
Their loved ones for to greet.

Christmas is a big day
With dramas – midnite song
And when believers strong in faith
Go out and tell the throng.

To some it's just a big day
No thought of Jesus' birth
Just following tradition
And varied forms of mirth.

Christmas is a big day
We hope its big to you
Not just big tradition – wise

But big with meaning too.

For Christmas is a special day
A day to worship One
Who out of love for fallen man
Sent forth his only Son. †

Only One
1972

An Angel
God has innumerable angels
Who follow His command
But only Gabriel was sent to Mary blest as planned.

A Light
Firelights flicked in the fields
Lanterns gleamed reward
But only one light shone forth
The glory of the Lord.

A Star
Millions of heavenly lights
twinkled in the sky
But only one bright guiding star
Could princes verify.

A Baby
Many babies born that night
Whom Herod later slew
But only One of Bethlehem's babes
Was spared to lives renew.

A King
Caesars, Herods lived and died
To God and man ignore
But only one King came to die
To live forevermore.

A Savior
Saviors come and saviors go
To nations in distress
But only One was born to save
All men in sin's depress. †

Christmas in Larkana

1973

Christmas in Larkana in seventy-three
With cards and lights and a silver tree
Making cookies and candy and fruit cake too
With rationed sugar – a problem or two.

No snow on the ground or frost in the air
But plenty of chilly evenings to spare
We'll light our heater on the eve of Yule
Carolers come last to our house as a rule.

After hot tea and biscuits and more to eat
To a midnight service we'll all retreat
To sing and pray and remember His birth
Who came to save men all over the earth.

On Christmas morn at the appointed time
Christians gather to worship on a day sublime
Dressed for the day in new array
To celebrate Christmas – to all a "Big Day".

Visits and homes all whitewashed and clean
And decorated brightly – a holiday scene
Colored streamers and lights and greetings from afar
A desert bough and a silver star.

From huts remote near the Indus bed
Mar Waris will come who to Christ have fled
To worship in town on Christ's birthday
And to share in the joy of His new way.

The day after Christmas, as in years before
The young folks have a picnic in store
To the ruins of Moenjodaro we'll go
For a day of fun and food – but no snow.

On the twenty seventh at three afternoon
We'll meet for our jelsa-games and a tune
Races and contests – we'll have a ball
With the giving of gifts to kids and all.

Again we'll meet on New Year's eve
Living room will be crowded, I do believe
To fellowship together in Christ our Lord
Into seventy-four with the Living Word. †

God Could Have Made Another Way
Furlough, 1975

God could have made another way
To give salvation's plan
But by His grace and perfect love
He chose to come as man.

God could have made another way
Whereby the world to save
But by His grace and perfect love
Life on a cross he gave.

God could have made another way
To tell the world that's lost
But by His grace and perfect love
He chose to bear the cost. †

Light

"The people who walked in
darkness have seen a
Great Light." (Is. 9:2)

Light first came to earth
When from the living God
Came forth amazing words
"Let there be light."
(Gen. 1:3)

Light was given to earth
When from the living God
Came forth the royal law
His Light and Truth.
(Ps. 43:3)

Light encamped on earth
When from the living God
Came forth in brilliancy
His shekinah glory.
(Ex. 40:34)

Light has dwelt on earth
When from the living God
Came forth His only Son
The Light of the World.
(Jn. 8:12)

Light spreads o'er the earth
When from the living God
Are sent ambassadors
To bring His salvation.
(Acts 13:47)

Light will come to earth
When from the living God
Descends the holy city
Whose light is God's glory.
(Rev. 21:23) †

Shepherds - Angels
(Luke 2:8 – 20)

Shepherds in the fields
Keeping constant watch
Their flocks needed them
For it was night.

An angel came suddenly
God's glory encompassed them
They were afraid
The sky was bright

Then the angel spoke
"Don't be afraid
I bring good news of joy
And it is right"

"It is for all the people-
Today in David's town
A savior has been born
Messiah – the Light."

"The sign is this
The Babe is wrapped
In strips of cloth
Wound so very tight."

Angels – a great army
Suddenly appeared
Singing praise to God
Peace to men of right.

The angels left
Returning to heaven
Then the shepherds said
"We'll see this sight."

They hurried to Bethlehem
And found the Baby
Lying in the manger still
'Twas their delight.

The shepherds spread the word
About the child
Amazing all who had heard
They spread the light.

To their fields and work
The shepherds returned
With glory and praise to God
Oh what a night!

Like the shepherds
Let us tell the news
Like angels – let us praise God
Christ is the Light. †

Glory to God

1979

Glory to God
    In the highest
Sounded forth
    From the heavenly host
On that first Christmas night. (Lk 2:14)

Glory to God
    And praise to Him
A testimony
    By the poor shepherds
As they returned amazed. (Lk. 2:20)

Glory to God
    Who is our only Savior
Now and forever
    Majesty power and authority
Through Jesus Christ our Lord. (Jude 25)

Glory to God
    And peace in heaven
For the Blessed King comes
    In the name of the Lord
With joy the disciples cried. (Lk. 19:38)

Glory to God
    Forever and ever
For He is the only God
    Eternal, immortal and invisible
He is King. Amen. (I Tim 1:17)

Glory to God
    The only wise
Forever, through Jesus Christ
    Revealed in the gospel
That all nations might believe and obey. (Rom. 16:25 – 27) †

Jesus Came!

1980

Jesus Came
    He came to show
The love of God
    To men on earth below.

Jesus Came
    He came to speak
The words of God
    All men should seek.

Jesus Came
    He came to love
As none else could
    In earth or heav'n above.

Jesus Came
    He came to be
God in the flesh
    God from eternity.

Jesus Came
    He came to give
A perfect life – in death
    That we might live.

Jesus Came
    He came to die
For you, for me
    And all who know not why.

Jesus Came
    He came to change
A sinner such as I
    In a world so strange.

Jesus Came
    He came to live
In human hearts
    New life to give. †

When I Think of Christmas...
1983

Christmas makes me think of Jesus
    Born in Bethlehem long ago,
    Born to come and save His people
    And to them God's image show.

Christmas makes me think of family
    One time gathered in our home,
    But now so many miles apart
    In diff'rent places 'neath the earth's dome.

Christmas makes me think of carols
    Sung from hearts made warm by love,
    Sung in churches, homes and ghettos
    Echoing sounds from heav'n above.

Christmas makes me think of giving
    Sharing gifts with those you love,
    Sharing joy with those who need it
    Inspired in deed by Heaven's Dove.

Christmas makes me think of starlight
    Shining o'er old Bethlehem's town
    Shining ever in the heavens
    Telling man God's love came down.

Christmas makes me think of "Big Day"
    That's the word we know so well,
    That's the word with depth of meaning
    God came down on earth to dwell.

Christmas makes me think of missions
    Sending out the gospel light,
    Sending forth those called as servants
    To tell good news in darkest night.

Christmas makes me think of you...
 Joy this day...
  And the whole year through. †

God Became Man
(Colossians 1:15 – 23)

1984

Who was born in Judah's town
Whose birth all Christians claim?
Was he just another man
Destined to rise to fame?

God's likeness became visible
In Christ his firstborn Son
He is supreme and over all
And with the Father, One.

All things by Him God did create
Which were unseen and seen
Powers, rulers, mighty thrones
On earth and heav'n serene.

By Him and for Him all was made
All things He is before
And in Him all things take their place
His honor is much more.

Of the Church he is the Head
The One god first has raised
From death, that in all He may be
Supreme; may God be praised.

In Him God's fullness was to dwell
This was the Father's will
And in Him God did reconcile
All things by sin made ill.

God has made peace through His One Son
Where He, upon the cross

Shed His blood for men like me
Without Him, what a loss.

So we who once were enemies
In conduct and in will
Have now become His holy friends
This Gospel is hope still. †

What If there Were no Christmas?
1985

What if there were no Christmas
That happy time of the year
When 'round the world both old and young
Are filled with joy and cheer.

What if there were no Angels
To announce a holy birth
From a glory filled eastern sky
Reaching down from heav'n to earth.

What if there were no shepherds
To receive good news of joy
That God had sent the Savior Christ
Who was born a baby boy.

What if there were no wise men
To travel from afar
Who came to worship a new King
Led by a brilliant star.

What if there were no Mary
And Joseph her husband true
With courage and with upright hearts
They did what God told them to.

What if there were no Jesus
God's son born so poor and weak
Who came to save us from our sins
And blessed the poor and meek.

What if there were no Bible
With its words of faith and love
To reveal to us a message true
From a God Who reigns above.

What if there were no Gospel
To share with a broken world
No news of a Redeemer's love
To poor lost sinners hurled.

But if there were no Christmas
No Savior – no Christ to love
Life would be filled with empty hope
On earth and heaven above.

Thank God there is a Christmas
And a Christ Who came to save
And a living hope for a sinful race
We have life, because God gave. †

Christmas in Pakistan

1986

"What do you do at Christmas?"
Some people often ask.
"In what way do you celebrate?
What is your yuletide task?"
        Some things we do are common
        To Christians the world around
        Like baking cookies, cakes and pies
        And fruit cake by the pound.
We have no snow or evergreens
Or lighted shopping malls
But we have lights and strung up cards
And friends who make house calls.
        Our loved ones are so far away
        We miss them very much
        But at this season of the year
        They're sure to keep in touch.
And in their place a family
Of fellow missionaries
Join together in Christmas fun
The food, it always varies.
        No turkey here, but chicken or goose
        Grace the dining table
        With trimmings full from east and west
        We feast, it is no fable.
We share gifts with young and old
With friends and servants, too
For Christmas is a giving time
And to give is nothing new.
        Carol parties come and sing
        They're out all Christmas Eve
        They come at seven, or eleven
        With joy we them receive.
This year the church will have a meal
For the fellowship of all

And gifts to all the children there,
A plastic toy or ball.
                Through special books and tracts and teas
                We share the Gospel story
                With Muslim friends who often ask
                Of the One who came from glory.
On Christmas Day we'll go to church
And hear the message true
In another tongue and another way
Good News for Pakistan, too.
                Now to end these dozen lines
                Is a task not hard to do.
                With Christmas light and joy and peace
                Our love is sent to you. †

Who was this Child?

Who was this child
Born to a poor Jewish girl
In Bethlehem of Judea so long ago?

He was in very nature God
Yet did not grasp at this equality
But made Himself nothing.

He humbled Himself still further
And obediently accepted death
Even the death of the cross.

Because of this, God exalted Him
To the highest place and
Gave Him a name above all.

His name is Jesus and
Every knee should bow to Him
And every tongue should confess Him

God the Father is glorified
When all creation bows and proclaims
Jesus Christ is Lord.

He is no longer a child in a manger
But forever the God-man
Exalted in heaven.

        We love Him
        We worship Him
        We serve Him
        We watch for Him
        This advent season.
        Phil 2:6 – 11 †

Separation at Christmas

Christmas is a time of family gatherings
   In the home with gladness
      United with loved ones
         The joy of togetherness
            With others to share.
But Christmas is also a time
   Of separation – loneliness
      Often at great distance
         From those you love
            For whom you care.
God the Son knew the pains
   Of separation from the Father's presence
      And the glorious mansions
         To take upon Himself
            The form of man to share.
Mary and Joseph knew the cost
   Of separation from home and friends
      To travel to a Judean town
         Which had no room for the Virgin
            Her firstborn to bear.
The shepherds knew the meaning
   Of separation when they were left
      In the darkness
         By the radiant Heavenly Host
            But they took to heart the message
               And glorified God there.
The wise men knew the results
   Of separation from home and hearth
      To travel over barren hills
         To find the King of Kings
            They knew not where.
At Christmas time when you and I
   Come to feel the tug of separation
      From those we love so dear

Remember we are not alone
Others too had hearts laid bare
With them we share. †

Remember Christ at Christmas

Whose birth do we remember
    This season of the year?
He's One descended from the first
    Like us, Son of Adam.

It's good that we remember
    At this glad Christmas time
That from the Father of faith
    Came one true Son of Abraham.

All nations should remember
    This year and every year
That through a kingly line
    Was born the Son of David.

Come, let us all remember
    At this year's advent time
A virgin bore by Spirit's power
    A child, the son of Mary.

We gladly do remember
    As Christmas bells ring out
The one who came to seek and save
    Was surely son of Man.

The world must e'er remember
    As Christmas comes and goes
That Jesus born as Christ the Lord
    Is Eternal Son of God. †

His Place and Ours
1988

Christ left His place of glory
    To come to a sinful place
        A world estranged from God

The Prophet told of a place
    Where the Ruler would be born
        A place long chosen by God

There was no place for Jesus
    In ancient Bethlehem's Inn
        No place for the Son of God

The Messiah had no place
    That He could call His home
        And He was the Son of God

To a place called Calvary
    Our Savior went one day
        To bring us back to God

He's gone to prepare a place
    For those who trust in Him
        Forever with our God

In times of stress and strain
    There is a place for saints
        A hiding place in God

As we leave our place in Pakistan
    Where we've lived and served for years
        We need to trust our God †

What is Christmas?

1989

Christmas is Uniting
With family ad friends,
And fellow believers –
Christ the Lord has come.

Christmas is Remembering
Caroling in the snow –
Singing 'round the piano
With loved ones now gone Home.

Christmas is Praying
For loved ones
Home and Overseas,
Colleagues – churches – friends.

Christmas is Praising
God in the highest heaven
With the heavenly armies
- Peace to those who please Him.

Christmas is Singing
Carols centuries old
And songs of recent years
Glory to God with the voice.

Christmas is Giving
Not reluctantly or under compulsion
For God loves a cheerful giver.

Christmas is Receiving
The greatest Gift ever
God's son – eternal life
- the right to become God's children.

Christmas is Hoping
For peace on earth
And peace in human hearts –
For the coming of the Prince of Peace.

Christmas is Laughing
With little children, big ones too
In the snow – on the floor –
'neath the tinseled tree.

Christmas is Crying

As one remembers former years
And loneliness builds up
To bring forth tears.

Christmas is Loving
And because God loved and gave
We learn something of how
We need to love and give.

Christmas is Sharing
The gifts of life and love
With those we love
And those who need our love.

Christmas is Proclaiming
To a world so mired in sin
That Christ and Christ alone
Is Savior, King and Lord. †

Christmas is a Time for Singing
1991

The angels sang a song and so do we
    As we gather with loved ones around the tree.
The song's not only for one place or time
    But it resounds in many a land and clime.
The song is sung in homes and open space
    In hospitals and in the market place.
The song is sung and loved in nursing home
    Where joy is found in simple song or poem.
Through audio cassette the song comes clear
    In a Karachi hotel – Islam so very near.
Through the air waves of a Muslim land
    The song sounds clear in tongues men understand.
And on a clear and cold December eve
    Through carol voices homes much joy receive.
On Christmas Day till the hours are done
    We celebrate the birth of God's own Son.
And the song we sing is the angels' song
    Glory to God in heaven and peace to right all wrong.
A Savior is born today for all of you
    He is Christ the Lord, and this is true! †

"And He will be called… Price of Peace. Of the increase of His government and peacethere will be no end." (Is 9:7)

1992

No end to His peace
For He is the Prince of Peace.
No end to His peace
For the Lord blesses His people with peace. (Ps. 29:11)
No end to His peace
For He promises peace to His saints. (Ps. 85:8)
No end to His peace
For He keeps in perfect peace the one who trusts in Him. (Is. 26:3)
No end to His peace
For He has made a covenant of peace. (Is. 54:10)
No end to His peace
For He guides into the path of peace. (Lk. 1:79)
No end to His peace
Upon whom His favor rests. (Lk. 2:14)
No end to His peace
For Jesus said, "in Me you may have peace." (Jn. 16:33)
No end to His peace
For "My peace I give you." (Jn. 14:27)
No end to His peace
For he made peace through His blood shed on the cross. (Col. 1:20, Eph. 2:14 – 18)
No end to His peace
"Let the peace of Christ rule in your hearts." (Col 3:15) †

What does Christmas Mean to Me?
1998

What does Christmas mean to me?
Could it be bright lights or an evergreen tree?
Or presents and wrapping,
    Shopping and feasting,
Hearing music that touches the ears and heart,
    And singing carols years have set apart?
Or meeting with loved ones and
    Friends, some from afar
Or gazing at night at a winter star?

Christmas means all that to me
But so much more, oh don't you see?
Christmas means that I in my sin
Have a Savior who was born,
    And who dwells within
This heart of mine which had no hope.
For without His love and saving grace,
I was lost and condemned to the darkest place.
Christmas means so much to me
    That I see the cross in each Christmas tree. †

What Will the New Year Bring?

2000

What will the New Year bring?
We do not know.
But we do know and trust
That the God of our salvation
Will carry on His good work
      To completion
And in this Hope we
Wait for the Day of Christ Jesus. (Phil. 1:6) †

Christmas Carols

2005

We sing with words old melodies
Which bring to us fond memories.
The music touches many a heart
But what of the words, do they have a part?

Do people think and understand
That God Himself came to this land
And in the form of a babe – a Son
Born of a virgin, sin's curse He won?

As the songs ring out at home or mall
From radio, TV or DVD stall
Does the truth sink in, or does it pass one by
That the King of Kings was born to die?

Let's sing the words with faith and thought
And remember the miracle God has wrought
To save us sinners and make us whole
In a world so lost and out of control. †

One Message – One Word
2007

The message for the world
>> Is the message of joy
>>>> The word for you and for me.

The message to shepherds
>> At night in the fields
>>>> A word of God's good news.

The message to Mary
>> A young Jewish virgin
>>>> Was a word of miracle.

The message to Joseph
>> A noble and righteous man
>>>> Was a word about a Savior.

The message to wise men
>> Traveling from the east
>>>> Was a word through a star.

The message to Simeon
>> Devout and waiting long
>>>> Was a word of light and glory.

The message to Anna
>> A fasting and praying saint
>>>> Was a word of thanks and redemption.

The message of Christmas
>> Is that of Immanuel
>>>> The Word – "God with us." †

The Incarnation

2008

To fearful Zechariah the angel of the Lord came,
   his message was to parents in old age-
      a child would be born to be great
         and turn people in **preparation**.

To a young virgin Mary in Galilee's town of Nazareth
   the angel Gabriel appeared
      and startled her that whe would
         bear God's Son – a special **annunciation**.

To Elizabeth the Holy Spirit moved
   to stir the babe in her womb
      so she blessed her visiting relative Mary
         in an act of **jubilation**.

To Mary's soul and spirit came
   a song of glory and rejoicing
      to the Mighty One whose mercy
         is from **generation** to **generation**.

To the lowly shepherts in Bethlehem's fields
   watching sheep at night
      there came an angel with good news and a multitude
         of the heavenly host shining the
            glory of the the Lord in terifying **illumination**.

To the wise men from eastern lands
   arose a guiding star to lead them
      to the child King's house and
         bowing in worship gave gifts of **dedication**.

To aged Simeon, righteous and devout,
   was revealed by the Holy Spirit
      the child he held was God's salvation

and Israel's **consolation.**

To Anna a prophetess from a little known tribe
   who never left the temple in her widowhood
      was given the recognition
         that Jesus was Israel's **redemption.**

To you and me, year by year
   the Christmas story is told, old but new,
      for by faith in the baby Jesus we
         experience God's **revelation** and His **salvation.** †

Pain at Christmas

2009

The Father suffered pain
>In sending His only Son
>Into a world which would
>Ultimately reject him

The Son suffered pain
>In leaving heaven's glories
>And His Father's home
>To live a homeless life

Mary and Joseph suffered pain
>In bearing ridicule
>From friends and relatives
>Because of a strange pregnancy

Hundreds of mothers suffered pain
>When a very cruel king
>Ordered that their babies
>Be killed in Bethlehem.

The Holy Family suffered pain
>In traveling to a strange land
>To spare the new-born King
>From Herod's brutal slaughter

At Christmas time
>Amidst the joy of family and friends
>Many suffer the pain
>Of separation, loneliness and heartache.

The world is filled with pain
>So much who can endure
>It waits Redemption's Day
>When Christ will bring the cure

When we suffer pain
>> In body soul and spirit
>> It reminds us of the One
> Who knows what pain truly is.

And so I must endure
>> This temporary pain
>> For it will surely end
> In God's own time and plan.

I Peter 5:10 "And the God of all grace, who called you to his eternal glory in Christ, after you have suffered a little while, will himself restore you and make you strong, firm and steadfast." †